FOREST FARE

Studying Food Webs in the Forest

JULIE K. LUNDGREN

Rourke

Publishing LLC

Vero Beach, FL 32964
rourkepublishing.com

www.rourkepublishing.com

Project Assistance:
The author thanks Gwendolyn Hooks, Tracy Nelson Maurer, and the team at Blue Door Publishing.

Photo credits:
Cover Photos: Forest © szefei, Jaguar © Daniel Hebert, Black Caiman © Warwick Lister-Kaye, Capybara © Alistair Michael Thomas, Grass © Lim Yong Hian; Page 4 © Alexander M. Omelko; Page 5 © Galyna Andrushko. Hydromet, Sharon D, Juerg Schreiter; Page 6 © Dmitry Naumov; Page 7 © Christopher Meder; Page 8 © Vicki Franc; Page 9 © flickr; Page 10 © Kato Inowe. Timur Kulgarin; Page 11 © Bryant Jayme; Page 12 © South12th Photography, Michael Maggs; Page 13 © TTphoto; Page 14 © Quest786, Sharon D; Page 15 © Tim Jenner, Dr. Morley Read, Engineer111; Page 16 © Daniel Hebert, Joy Brown; Page 17 © Dennis Donohue; Page 18 © Timothy Craig Lubcke; Page 19 © faberfoto, Dr. Morley Read; Page 20 © Michael Fritzen, Melissa Dockstader; Page 21 © mashe; Page 22 © Daniel Hebert, Engineer111, Dr. Morley Read, Lupo, Dmitrijs Mihejevs, Drahomír Kalina, Joshua Haviv, TZajaczkowski, Alistair Michael Thomas, VR Photos, Timothy Craig Lubcke, Christopher Meder, Barbara Ayrapetyan, slowfish, Lim Yong Hian, Dmitry Rukhlenko, Dr. Morley Read, Joseph Calev, Dr. Morley Read, Sebastian Kaulitzki; Page 23 © Dennis Donohue; Page 24 © graham s. klotz; Page 25 © Peter von Bucher, Michael Woodruff; Page 26 © Leah-Anne Thompson; Page 27 © Daniel Hebert, Alvesgaspar; Page 28 © Maxim Petrichuk; Page 29 © Danijel Micka

Editor: Jeanne Sturm

Cover and page design by Nicola Stratford, Blue Door Publishing

Library of Congress Cataloging-in-Publication Data

Lundgren, Julie K.
  Forest fare : studying food webs in the forest / Julie K. Lundgren.
     p. cm. -- (Studying food webs)
  Includes index.
  ISBN 978-1-60472-316-8 (hardcover)
  ISBN 978-1-60472-781-4 (softcover)
  1. Forest ecology--Juvenile literature. 2. Food chains (Ecology)--Juvenile literature. 3. Forest--Juvenile literature. I. Title.
  QH541.5.F6L86 2009
  577.3'16--dc22

Printed in the USA

CG/CG

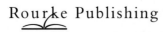

Rourke Publishing

www.rourkepublishing.com – rourke@rourkepublishing.com
Post Office Box 3328, Vero Beach, FL 32964

Table Of Contents

On The Cover

Jaguars prey on many different animals, including caimans.

Caimans hunt animals that come to the river's edge to drink.

Capybaras nibble on grasses, aquatic plants, and fruits.

Grasses provide food for forest herbivores.

Strands in a Web

All life needs sunlight, water, air, and food. Green plants change light from the Sun into food energy through **photosynthesis**. Plants use the food to live and grow. When an animal eats the plant, the energy passes to the animal, and passes again when the animal is eaten. This energy pathway from one living thing to another is a **food chain**. Since organisms are part of many food chains, all the food connections in an area compose a **food web**.

Like threads in a spider's web, food chains interconnect and support one another.

CHEW ON THIS

Plants use water, carbon dioxide, and chlorophyll to change sunlight into a simple sugar.

Food chains begin with sunlight and end with an animal.

Natural Forest Networks

An area's plants and animals and the ways they interact with each other and the land define an **ecosystem**. Climate and the availability of resources, like food and water, determine the kinds and numbers of species. Forests grow in many climates. Tropical forests are warm and moist all year. Leafy, or deciduous, trees handle seasonal temperature changes in temperate forests. Temperate forests grow between equatorial rainforests and northern boreal forests. Boreal forests are without frost only 50 to 100 days each year.

General distribution of boreal forests

General distribution of tropical rainforests

Forest Fare

Green Machines

Forest plants, the **primary producers**, generate food from sunlight. They use carbon dioxide and give off oxygen for animals and people to breathe. Plants provide the food web foundation in their leaves, stems, bark, roots, seeds, flowers, and fruit.

Forests are structured in layers. The top layer, or canopy, receives the most sunlight and wind. The next layer down is the understory, where bushes and young trees grow in dappled light. The still forest floor shelters plants with the ability to grow in shade. In the tropics, a fourth layer, the emergent layer, pokes up taller than the canopy. Emergent trees serve as watchtowers and restaurants for eagles, monkeys, and butterflies.

Where sunlight pierces the canopy, seedlings sprout.

The emergent layer and canopy form a green roof over the tropical forest.

In tropical forests, vines seeking sunlight snake up trees. Bromeliads collect water in their leafy centers. Tree frogs and insects lay eggs in these miniature aquariums. The dark forest floor and poor soil defeat most seedlings. Instead, plants sprout in sunny tree branches. The moist air and frequent rains supply needed water.

Daily rainfall refreshes the center pools of each bromeliad.

CHEW ON THIS

More than 200 tree species can grow in 2.5 acres (one hectare) of rainforest.

Deciduous trees, like maples, oaks, birch, and basswood, dominate temperate forests. Temperate forests grow in areas with seasonal changes in daylight and temperature. These changes cause the trees to lose their leaves and go into a time of **dormancy** during the coldest, darkest days of the year. Animals living here must have **adaptations** to the lack of fresh, green food during the winter.

CHEW ON THIS

In autumn, chlorophyll in leaves fades, revealing red and gold colors.

Fantasy Forest

In rare, ancient temperate rainforests in the western United States, daring biologists climbed the world's tallest living trees and found a forest in miniature. In the branches, crevices, and hollows of each massive treetop, soil collected over thousands of years. Huckleberry bushes, small trees, lichens, ferns, insects, lizards, and birds form an ecosystem in the air.

Fungi soak up water and nutrients. Algae perform photosynthesis. The two join to form lichens.

Redwood National Park, California

SACRAMENTO

SAN FRANCISCO

LOS ANGELES

SAN DIEGO

The world's tallest tree, named Hyperion, touches the clouds at 378.1 feet (115.2 meters) tall. A person on a skyscraper's 37th floor sees from the same height as a bird on top of Hyperion. Hyperion stands in Redwood National Park.

Boreal forests contain hardy plants and trees able to withstand fierce winters.

The boreal forest blankets the northern latitudes with firs, pine, spruce, and tamarack. Lichens, moss, and fallen tree needles carpet the forest floor and often frozen soil. Except for tamaracks, conifers keep their leaves in order to save energy. The dark, waxy needles absorb the Sun's heat efficiently and limit water loss. Trees here have a cone shape, the better to shed snow from their branches.

Animal Menus

Plant eaters, or herbivores, are **primary consumers**, the first animals in food chains. Animals have adaptations for eating plants. Rodent incisors, or front teeth, grow continuously. With each bite of tough stems and seeds, the top teeth rub past the bottom teeth, sharpening them like razors. Herbivores help plants, too. As animals browse, seeds latch onto their fur. Later the seeds fall onto new ground. Fruit eaters also spread plant seeds in their waste.

CHEW ON THIS

In early spring in temperate forests, gray squirrels lick the sweet sap that runs down sugar maples.

The long, curved bill of this hummingbird plumbs flowers rich in nectar.

Carnivores eat other animals. Those who eat primary consumers are **secondary consumers**. With excellent vision and webbed feet, South American bush dogs fish from riverbanks by submerging their heads. Top predators amaze with their stealth and power. Harpy eagles wing through the canopy to pick off unwary monkeys, sloths, and snakes. Jaguars' jaws crush the skulls of their prey. **Omnivores**, like orangutans, consume both animals and plants.

Orangutan mothers teach their young where and when to find more than 300 kinds of fruit.

Velvet worms douse prey with sticky glue, inject digestive juices, and then suck up the resulting soup.

Harpy eagles grip large prey with powerful feet. Their talons compare in size to the claws of a brown bear.

Temperate forest secondary consumers include shrews, bats, weasels, and hawks. Swift, adaptable coyotes relish fruits and berries, frogs, insects, and plants, in addition to rabbits, small rodents, and birds. Like others in the dog family, coyotes feed on **carrion**, too. Other omnivores, like raccoons, foxes, and black bears, sometimes raid dog food, bird feeders, small livestock, and garbage if they live near people.

CHEW on THIS

In areas of poor soil, carnivorous plants like sundews digest insects for extra nutrition.

This red fox has managed to catch a gray squirrel for its dinner.

Boreal carnivores use special adaptations to hunt successfully. The expert ears of great gray owls can detect mice tunneling beneath 2 feet (61 centimeters) of snow. Martens slink among branches pursuing squirrels and birds. At the food chain's summit, gray wolves work together to take down large herbivores, like deer and caribou.

To save energy, sloths slowly chew leaves and fruit, and nap often.

Power Lunch

Food webs show the energy flow from one organism to another. At every step in the food chain, living things store incoming energy in their growing bodies. As one thing eats another and energy moves up the food chain, it shrinks. Why? Not all the energy is stored. Animals and plants spend some energy performing daily activities. Animals only pass on the energy stored as body weight. This decreasing energy flow means ecosystems can support many plants, some herbivores, and only a few top predators.

Canopy bridges allow people to experience life high in the trees.

Studying Food Webs

How do scientists learn about food webs? Good eyes and patience! Watching plants and animals is simplest. To observe canopy activity, field workers have used construction cranes, rope bridges and ladders, and even blimps, to rise above the ground.

Ecologists examine owl pellets to learn what owls eat. Owl pellets form in the bird's crop, a pocket in the digestive system in the lower throat. The muscular crop grinds the meal before it passes to the stomach. Owls cough out a slimy clump of indigestible teeth, fur, and bones.

Clean-Up Time

In nature, nothing goes to waste. Not fallen leaves, old logs, or leftovers from a kill. Scavengers come by first for an easy meal. Then **decomposers** break down the forest litter into nutrients plants can use again. Fungi, bacteria, and algae all play a part in forest housekeeping. Microscopic bacteria decompose animal waste and carrion. Decomposition occurs quickest when it's warm and damp.

Standing dead trees provide animals with nesting cavities, hunting and feeding platforms, and feasts of insects and grubs.

Fungi, like mushrooms and mold, rot wood and other tough plant material.

CHEW ON THIS

Earthworms process tons of dead leaves into rich soil. Harness the power of worms to transform fruit and vegetable scraps into soil by constructing your own earthworm compost bin.

jaguars

harpy eagles

velvet worms

reptiles

South American
bush dogs

fish

tapirs

insects

rodents

small fish

sloths

leaves

fruit and
nuts

nectar,
flowers

grasses &
seeds

aquatic
plants

ENERGY FLOW

beetles

sow bugs

fungi

bacteria

In a food web, a large foundation of producers supports the consumers with energy from the Sun. As energy is spent on its way to the top, fewer animals can be supplied with enough energy to meet their needs. Decomposers recycle food web waste from all food levels.

Top Predators
jaguars, harpy eagles

Secondary Consumers (Carnivores and Omnivores)
velvet worms, reptiles such as snakes, lizards, caiman, and iguanas, South American bush dogs, fish

Primary Consumers (Herbivores)
tapirs, insects, capybaras and other rodents, small fish, sloths, and monkeys

Primary Producers (Plants)

Decomposers
beetles, sow bugs, fungi, bacteria

Out of Balance

A growing world population demands more food, fuel, lumber, and mining products. Forest sections are often sold off from the whole for development or harvest. Fragmentation of large stretches of undeveloped forestland threatens animals of the inner forest. Animals sensitive to human activity may die off or move away when faced with noise, traffic, and lights.

Songbirds of the forest interior, like black and white warblers, face more predators when their neighborhood shrinks. Pets, raccoons, and crows, more numerous on forest edges, are better able to reach the interior of small forest patches.

After the timber harvest, bulldozers push aside the leftovers.

CHEW on THIS

As forests shrink, Earth's ability to protect its climate decreases. The carbon stored in forests is released, making climate change worse.

Deforestation, the removal of trees from an area, can have effects that last a long time. Tropical rainforests hold their nutrients in their plants and animals, not the soil. Crops planted on cleared land exhaust the thin topsoil in just a few years. Rainforests rarely grow again on abandoned farmland. Deforestation affects boreal and temperate forests, too. Young forests differ from forests that have been growing and developing over centuries. Some animals and plants appear only in mature forests. Ecologists struggle to understand the relationships and inhabitants of ancient forests before they disappear.

EARTH'S FEVER

Earth's average temperature is rising. Global warming causes climate change worldwide. Why? Huge amounts of carbon dioxide, a **greenhouse gas**, are being released into the atmosphere. Just as the glass walls of a greenhouse let in heat and light, then trap that heat, so do greenhouse gases. Most of the carbon dioxide comes from burning **fossil fuels**, like oil, coal, and natural gas. Fossil fuels heat homes, power cars, and provide electricity.

Climate change threatens plants and animals in complex ways. Boreal gray jays don't migrate. Instead they rely on cold weather to keep their berry and insect stashes fresh. With warmer autumn weather each year, their natural freezers fail and the food rots. This leaves them without food to last until spring.

Pesticides, the chemicals used to control insects, affect food webs. The pesticide DDT moves into all levels of the food web. It causes birds to lay eggs with thin shells. The fragile eggs break when birds try to incubate them. Because of DDT and other pollutants, bald eagles became **endangered** in the 1960s. In 1972, the United States outlawed DDT. Over the next 30 years, through teamwork by many governments and organizations, bald eagles recovered.

People need to balance their needs with the needs of nature. Stewardship means caring for something for the greater good. Being a good steward requires hard choices. Solving problems like global warming calls for solid detective skills. Recycling, composting, and buying products that use recycled paper are all actions that contribute to a healthier world.

Countries still use DDT as a cheap, efficient control for the mosquitoes that spread malaria, a dangerous blood disease. In countries that no longer use DDT, health officials worry about malaria outbreaks.

Visiting and learning about forests is another important step in stewardship. Many people practice ecotourism, or traveling to experience Earth's astounding natural places. Picture crossing rope bridges in the rainforest canopy, snowshoeing through a boreal bog in search of great gray owls, or hiking by moonlight through a temperate forest to a coyote's song. As people gain appreciation and understanding of Earth's incredible forests, their desire to protect them will grow.

CHEW ON THIS

The old saying "Put litter in its place!" today means recycling anything that can possibly be recycled. Consider taking home that empty soda can if a recycling bin isn't available.

Tree planting increases Earth's ability to reduce greenhouse gases.

Glossary

adaptations (ad-ap-TAY-shunz): ways of survival that animals and plants have to fit their environment

carrion (KAIR-ee-yon): bodies of dead animals

decomposers (dee-cum-POH-zerz): animals and plants that cause rot and decay, enriching the soil with valuable nutrients

dormancy (DOR-muhn-see): a time of temporary inactivity when biological processes slow to a bare minimum

ecosystem (EE-koh-sis-tum): the relationships between all the plants and animals and the place in which they live

endangered (en-DAYN-jerd): at risk of becoming extinct

food chain (FOOD CHAYN): a series of plants and animals, each of which is eaten by the one after it

food web (FOOD WEHB): in an ecosystem, the intricate network of food chains

fossil fuels (FAH-suhl FYOO-uhls): stored energy formed millions of years ago from the remains of plants and animals

greenhouse gas (GREEN-howss GAS): a gas in Earth's atmosphere that adds to the greenhouse effect and global warming

omnivores (AHM-nih-vorz): animals that feed on a wide variety of foods including both plants and animals

photosynthesis (foh-toh-SIN-thuh-siss): the process by which green plants transform the Sun's energy into food

primary consumers (PRYE-mair-ee kahn-SOO-merz): herbivores, the animals that eat primary producers

primary producers (PRYE-mair-ee proh-DOO-serss): plants that perform photosynthesis

secondary consumers (SEHK-uhn-dair-ee kahn-SOO-merz): animals that eat herbivores

Further Reading

Hungry for more? Your local library serves up additional information about forest ecology and food webs. Whet your appetite with these books and websites.

Books

Fleisher, Paul. *Forest Food Webs (Early Bird Food Webs).* Lerner Publications, 2007.

Morgan, Ben and Thomas Marent (photographer). *Rainforest.* DK Adult, 2006.

O'Donnell, Liam. *Understanding Photosynthesis with Max Axiom, Super Scientist.* Graphic Library, 2007.

Websites

Boreal Songbird Initiative
www.borealbirds.org/index.shtml

Smithsonian National Zoological Park
nationalzoo.si.edu/Animals/Amazonia/Exhibit/

NatureWorks
www.nhptv.org/natureworks/default.htm

Index

About The Author

Julie K. Lundgren grew up near Lake Superior where she reveled in mucking about in the woods, picking berries, and expanding her rock collection. Her appetite for learning about the intricate details of nature led her to a degree in biology from the University of Minnesota. She currently lives in Minnesota with her husband and two sons.